World Crafts and Recipes

Recipe and Craft Guide to

GERMANY

Julia Harms

Mitchell Lane

P.O. Box 196
Hockessin, Delaware 19707
Visit us on the web: www.mitchelllane.com
Comments? Email us: mitchelllane@mitchelllane.com

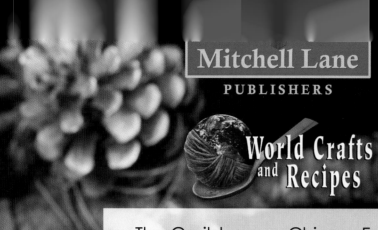

Mitchell Lane
PUBLISHERS

World Crafts and Recipes

The Caribbean • China • France
Germany • India • Indonesia
Israel • Italy • Japan • South Africa

PUBLISHER'S NOTE: The facts on which this book is based have been thoroughly researched. Documentation of such research can be found on page 60. While every possible effort has been made to ensure accuracy, the publisher will not assume liability for damages caused by inaccuracies in the data, and makes no warranty on the accuracy of the information contained herein.

To reflect current usage, we have chosen to use the secular era designations BCE ("before the common era") and CE ("of the common era") instead of the traditional designations BC ("before Christ") and AD (*anno Domini*, "in the year of the Lord").

EDITOR'S NOTE: As someone who usually doesn't like meat, I wasn't expecting to like many of the recipes in this book. I was surprised when my favorite recipe ended up being the Rouladen (and the amazing desserts, of course!). I hope you will enjoy exploring Germany through the recipes and crafts as much as I did, and that some of these foods might even become your own favorites!

Library of Congress Cataloging-in-Publication data
Harms, Julia.
 Recipe and craft guide to Germany / by Julia Harms.
    pages cm. — (World crafts and recipes)
 Audience: 9-13.
 Audience: Grade 7 to 8.
 Includes bibliographical references and index.
 ISBN 978-1-61228-300-5 (library bound)
 1. Cooking, German—Juvenile literature.
 2. Handicraft—Germany—Juvenile literature.
 I. Title.
 TX721.H355 2013
 641.5943—dc23
                                    2012041975
eBook ISBN: 9781612283746

Printing   1   2   3   4   5   6   7   8   9

PLB

CONTENTS

Fast cars driving at over 100 miles per hour along the autobahn, people drinking beer and eating sausages, romantic castles and cuckoo clocks, two World Wars and the Holocaust—these are just some of the things people think of when they hear "Germany." But did you know that the famous composers Johann Sebastian Bach, Ludwig van Beethoven, Wolfgang Amadeus Mozart, and Richard Wagner; writers Johann Wolfgang von Goethe, Friedrich Schiller, and Hermann Hesse; and philosophers Immanuel Kant, Georg Wilhelm Friedrich Hegel, and Friedrich Nietzsche were all German?

Germany is a democratic country in Central Europe. With 82 million inhabitants, it is the second-most populous country in Europe. Germany is slightly smaller than Montana, with 134,623 square miles (348,672 square kilometers) of land. The land is divided into sixteen states, called *Länder*. The capital city, Berlin, is also the country's largest with 3.4 million residents. The cities of Hamburg, Munich, and Cologne also have populations in the millions.

Germany's economy is the largest in the European Union, and the country is also one of the most important decision-makers in the Union.

The history of Germany can be confusing because its borders have changed over time. The land contained within modern-day German borders was at one time part of the Holy Roman Empire, Prussia, East Germany and West Germany, and other empires and countries throughout history.

The core area of Germany between the Rhine River in the West, the Baltic Sea in the North, and the Alps to the south has been settled by Germanic tribes since around 2000 BCE. In the first century BCE, Julius Caesar defined the concept of *Germania* when he wrote about the unconquered area east of the Rhine.

In 962 CE, Otto I became the first emperor of a unified medieval German state. This state was called the Holy Roman Empire, although it

Where in the World

never had anything to do with Rome or gladiators. The Middle Ages in the Holy Roman Empire were marked by growing cities and a general aversion to progress.

In the middle of the fourteenth century, the Black Death claimed millions of lives throughout Europe. Towards the end of the Middle Ages, in 1517, Martin Luther posted his *Ninety-Five Theses* on the door of the church of Wittenberg. This document criticizing the Catholic Church led to the creation of the Lutheran Church and other Protestant churches.

People in the northern states of the Holy Roman Empire were soon Protestant, while the residents of the southern states adhered to their Catholic beliefs. The two sides clashed in the Thirty Years' War (1618–

1648), one of the most violent wars Europe has ever seen. The result was that the central power of the Empire was divided among the states, so that they were almost independent.

At the beginning of the nineteenth century, citizens across Europe were increasingly unhappy with their governments. In 1848, European countries experienced uprisings as their citizens demanded democracy. Citizens hoping to unite all German-speaking lands into a single nation protested throughout Germany, but the Revolution failed.

In the meantime, the Industrial Revolution modernized the German economy and led to the rapid growth of cities. German universities became world-class centers for science and the humanities, while music and the arts flourished.

Unification of the many states was finally achieved when Prussian Chancellor Otto von Bismarck formed the German Empire in 1871. By the early 1900s, countries around the world had developed a complex system of alliances with one another. So when a group of Bosnians killed the heir to the Austrian throne in 1914, Austria's allies, including Germany, were brought into the dispute. This was the beginning of World War I.

After the First World War, Germany experienced a turbulent political and economic period which gave rise to the idea of Nazism which was anti-democratic, anti-semitic, and anti-communist. The growth of this ideology led to Adolf Hitler's rise to power. Not only was Hitler responsible for the Holocaust, during which approximately 6 million Jewish people were killed, but he also provoked the rest of world into World War II. Historians estimate that this war killed ten times as many people worldwide.

When the war ended, Germany was defeated and occupied, many of its cities destroyed, its people displaced and hungry. The country was split into two: East Germany and West Germany. West Germans resolved to never allow anything so horrendous to happen again, and adopted a new constitution which banned anti-semitism, created a safe haven for asylum seekers, and generally adopted democratic principles.

Partially to rebuild the country from the war damage, West Germany started to invite so-called *Gastarbeiter* (guest workers) from countries like Turkey, Greece, Italy, Spain, and Portugal in the 1950s. These workers often stayed and brought their families with them. Today Germany has over 7 million foreigners living within its territory, including approximately 1.5 million Turkish nationals.

Germany was also drawn into the Cold War, a dispute between the capitalist Western world, led by the United States, and the communist Eastern world, led by the Soviet Union. While West Germany sided with the Western countries, East Germany allied itself with the Soviet Union. The most heavily-guarded border between the two worlds ran right through East and West Germany: the Berlin Wall. When the Wall came down in 1989, it signified to the world that this war was finally coming to an end, and the two German nations were united again.

Germans have a reputation for lacking a sense of humor and being very serious and industrious people. It is true that many Germans like to think, reason, and work, but they also like to enjoy life. There are around 10,000 festivals every year in Germany, including the famous Oktoberfest in Munich. Other festivals include the Christmas Markets in Nuremberg, the Cologne Carnival, and the Love Parade in Berlin.

In their spare time, Germans like to travel, play sports (especially soccer), ride bicycles, go for walks, or get together in pubs. Germans love cultural activities and a huge number of people play musical instruments, listen to concerts, and visit museums or other cultural institutions.

Tips for the Kitchen

Read through the recipe—all the way—before you start.

Wear an apron to protect your clothes.

Wash your hands with warm water and soap before you start and after handling raw meat.

Be careful! Always get help from **an adult** when you are using the oven, the stovetop, or sharp knives. Use oven mitts to lift hot lids, baking sheets, and pans. Protect the counter with a trivet before you set down a hot container.

Clean up right away.

Once you've made a recipe successfully, you can experiment the next time. Change the ingredients. Use cranberries instead of raisins, or honey instead of sugar.

Finally, share your food with your friends and family. Seeing people enjoy your cooking is as much fun as enjoying it yourself!

Buchdruck
Gutenberg Book Press

Johannes Gutenberg, who lived in the city of Mainz in the early fifteenth century, was the inventor of the modern book press. Book production existed well before Gutenberg's time, but relied on the less efficient woodblock technique. With the woodblock process, a whole page of text or illustration was carved, colored, and then covered with paper. The paper was rubbed carefully to transfer the color from the woodblock onto the page. The genius of Gutenberg's invention was to split the text into its individual components, such as lower and

upper case letters, punctuation marks, and abbreviations. These individual items were then cast as mirror images and assembled to form words, lines, and pages. Gutenberg also improved the speed of the printing process by using a screw press that didn't require the rubbing of the page.

Overall, Gutenberg made so many improvements to book production that it immediately became cheaper and faster to print books. Printing exploded

in the decades after Gutenberg's inventions. Instead of being restricted to churches and monasteries, books could be printed for the general population.

The Gutenberg process was used for well over 400 years to produce books, newspapers, pamphlets, and other printed materials. You can make a small book, a birthday party invitation, or a greeting card using the Gutenberg technique.

Materials

Bicycle tire inner tube (available at any store that sells
   bicycles or bicycle parts)
Corks (as many as you want to create letters and
   punctuation marks)
Very sharp scissors or Stanley knife
Glue
Ink or watercolor paints
Paper, cards, or whatever you want to print on
Cotton swabs

When using a Stanley
knife, please keep
fingers away from the
blade.

Instructions

1. With **adult** supervision, cut out the
   letters and any symbols or
   punctuation marks you want to
   use from the inner tube. Glue each
   one onto a cork, with the reverse

10

side facing up (so the letter is a mirror image of the letter you want to create).

2. Paint a letter with the ink or watercolors. You may have to use a cotton swab to clean excess color from around the letter.

3. Stamp the letter onto a scrap piece of paper to check how it comes out before printing on a card. You may have to adjust the amount of paint or the pressure you use to get the best results.

Maibaum
The Maypole

May 1 is a day to celebrate spring, especially in rural areas. The origins of this festival are not quite clear, whether they are Germanic (1800 BCE to 500 CE) or from a later period. But for many centuries this tradition has been going strong.

In modern times, Germans decorate a Maypole or May Tree. A young tree is cut down and its trunk is decorated with a crown of leaves and ribbons flying from the top or wrapped around the pole. The Maypole is carried around in a procession, then erected in the center of the village. Young people celebrate by dancing around the pole.

Many young romances originate on May 1 in Germany. In areas like Rhineland, Bergisches Land, Bavaria, Franconia, and Swabia, boys and young men also put a small Maypole in front of the house of the girl or woman that they like. A month later, the person who brought the tree will return to take it down again and, if his feelings are reciprocated, he will be given a gift or invited for a meal.

Materials

A 5-6 foot stick (this could be a straight branch from a tree, a stick from a craft shop, or even a broomstick)
2 small nails or thumbtacks
Heavy-duty stapler
Hammer
Ribbon in 2 different colors, each 10 feet long
Medium wire
Thin, soft wire
Pincer to cut the wire
A bunch of leafy twigs, each 1 foot long
Bucket filled with sand (optional)

1. Create the crown by constructing a circle with about 3 feet of wire. Cut two wires of the same length. Bend these wires over the circle in high arches at 90 degree angles to each other and attach them to the ring as shown in the diagram. Don't worry if the shape is not exactly right, the twigs will cover up any imperfections.

2. Attach the twigs to the wire crown with the thinner wire: all the way around the bottom circle and to the two arches. If you like, you can also wrap some additional ribbons around the wire crown or let some streak from the top of the crown once you have attached the crown to the pole.

3. With help from **an adult**, attach the ends of your two ribbons to the top of your pole with thumbtacks or nails. Wrap the ribbons around the pole. Attach the crown on top of the pole with a heavy-duty stapler.

4. Put your Maypole in a bucket filled with sand or a hole in the ground, and dance!

Rattenfänger von Hameln
The Pied Piper of Hamelin

The brothers Wilhelm and Jacob Grimm were researchers who hoped to capture the oral history and the legends of Germany and put them into writing. In the early nineteenth century, they published collections of German fairy tales and legends, making stories such as "Cinderella," "Sleeping Beauty," "Rumpelstilt-skin," and "Hansel and Gretel" popular. Many of these tales were later adapted into films by Disney, although the Disney versions were much less scary than the originals.

One of the tales was the story of the Pied Piper of Hamelin: in 1284 a man came to the town of Hamelin, promising the citizens to get rid of the rats. The citizens promised to pay him what he asked if he could really do what he promised. The pied piper took his pipe out of his colorful (or "pied") dress and started to play. Indeed, all the rats and mice came out from their hiding places and followed the pied piper who led them out of town and into the river where they drowned. When the citizens saw that he had done what he had promised, they changed their minds and didn't want to pay him anymore. The piper went away angry and returned soon after to play his pipe again —but this time it was the children of Hamelin who followed him. He led them out of town and they were never found again.

Nobody knows how much of this is fiction and how much is true.

Make a pipe or, technically, an oboe.

Thick drinking straw
Ruler
Pencil
Scissors (or a Stanley knife)

Instructions

1. If your straw has a bend in it, cut it off, so you only have a straight tube. Flatten out the top inch of the tube by pressing a ruler over it repeatedly to make the mouthpiece.
2. Cut the two creases of the mouthpiece off, about ½ to ¾ inch long, as shown. Blow hard into the straw to see if it makes a sound. If it does, continue to the next step. If not, try flattening the mouthpiece more, cutting the edges further, or changing the way you are positioning your lips until you are able to produce a sound from the straw.

When using a Stanley knife, please keep fingers away from the blade.

3. Lay the straw on your work surface and mark 4 holes along the top for the fingers. With **adult** supervision, cut out the holes with sharp scissors and play a melody!

German Technology

Germany has often been dubbed the land of thinkers. This is true for the German engineering field, too. Germany is famous for its research, inventions, and engineering, especially for its cars. Wilhelm Conrad Röntgen was a German scientist who won the Nobel Prize in Physics for his discovery of x-rays. Another German scientist, Daniel Gabriel Fahrenheit, invented precise thermometers and developed the Fahrenheit temperature scale still used today. The first diesel engine was built in Germany by Rudolf Diesel in 1897. More recently, Konrad Zuse invented the first programmable computer (the Z3) in 1941, and Karlheinz Brandenburg was instrumental in developing the MP3 format of music compression.

In many fields of engineering, Germany is still the market leader. There are some very big engineering companies such as Siemens and Krupp, and automotive manufacturers such as BMW, Porsche, Audi, and Mercedes. But most of the great craftsmanship and high-performance products are made by small and medium-sized family businesses distributed all over the country.

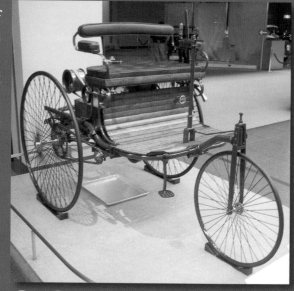

Benz Patent Motorwagen 1886 (Replica)

Make a classic German car using jet force technology.

Materials

Cardboard or light plastic, about 10 x 5 inches
Cardboard or light plastic for the wheels, about 6 x 6 inches
2 drinking straws
2 wooden skewers (available at your local grocery store)
10 inches of thread
The cap of a dishwashing liquid bottle, washed
Balloon
Cardboard or light plastic to make the body, about 10 x 15 inches
Scissors
Glue
Scotch tape
Sharp pencil

1. Cut out four wheels, each with a diameter of 1½– 2 inches. With the scissors, punch a small hole in the center of each wheel for the skewer to fit into tightly.

2. Glue the straws parallel to each other onto the 10 x 5 inch cardboard as shown, and allow the glue to dry completely. They should stick out from each side of the cardboard by about ½ inch.

The straws will hold the skewers, which will be the axles of the car. Cut the wooden skewers so that they poke out on each side of the straws by another ½ inch. Carefully attach the wheels to the skewers.

3. Insert the bottle top as deeply as possible into the balloon's neck, with the top facing out.

4. Attach the string to the base of the car with scotch tape as shown. Tie the balloon to the base with the string and point the

"exhaust" towards the back. Blow up the balloon and hold the exhaust shut with a finger. Position the car on a smooth surface and release your finger which will propel the car forward.

5. You can also make a body for your car from cardboard, but make sure it is big enough to hold the inflated balloon.

Make more than one and race them with your friends!

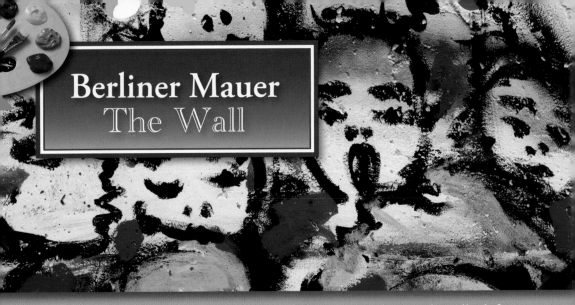

Berliner Mauer
The Wall

Germany lost the Second World War (1939–1945) to the Allied forces, including France, Britain, the Soviet Union, and the United States. The winning forces divided Germany into four zones, one for each country. Berlin, the capital at the time, was in the Soviet zone and was also divided into sectors between the occupying forces. In May of 1949 the Federal Republic of Germany (or West Germany) was created from the three zones occupied by capitalist forces: the United States, the United Kingdom, and France. In October of the same year, the German Democratic Republic (East Germany) was proclaimed in what had previously been the Soviet-occupied zone.

Throughout the 1950s, people from East Germany fled to West Germany in search of a better life or to be reunited with family. In order to keep people within its borders, the socialist East German government built a heavily-guarded wall around the three western sectors of Berlin and between East Germany and West Germany in 1961. Suddenly, families and neighbors in Berlin were divided by a wall of concrete that was supposed to "protect" the East Germans. The Wall was a symbol of the Cold War between the western capitalist nations and the eastern socialist ones.

Over time, the Wall became like a large canvas on which people expressed their anger over the division and the Cold War in words and pictures. When the war was over, and the two German nations were unified in 1989, people climbed onto the Wall and danced. When it was demolished, many took a piece of it home as a reminder of the symbol of the division of a nation.

Here we recreate graffiti on the Berlin Wall.

Paper
Large piece of cardboard or plywood
Grey paint
Pencil
Mask
Spray paint

Check with **an adult** before beginning this project. You will want to wear old clothes, and paint outside, or in an area protected with newspaper.

1. Sketch your graffiti design on a large piece of paper. We made a rainbow and the peace symbol.
2. Paint the cardboard or plywood cement grey, and allow the paint to dry. Draw your design lightly with a pencil. Wearing a mask, spray your design on the cardboard with spray paint.

Ostereier
Easter Eggs

Easter is a fun holiday—it arrives with the first signs of spring, and it often involves an Easter egg hunt with chocolates and small presents. The first mention of this tradition goes back to 1682.

In some regions, especially in the North, there are also huge Easter bonfires. Originally they were thought to drive out the winter and evil spirits; today they are mainly social gatherings. Many households also decorate a bush in the garden or a bunch of willow twigs with hollow decorated Easter eggs.

Materials

Chicken eggs
Pin
Bowl to blow egg contents into
Some toothpicks and a couple of wooden skewers
    (available at your local grocery store)
Scotch tape or blu-tack (adhesive putty)

Watercolor paint
Black marker
Colored embroidery thread or darning thread for hanging eggs
5 inches of thin wire
Toothpick

Willow, forsythia, peach or other twigs, at least 2 feet long
Large Vase

Instructions

1. Wash the eggs with dish soap and water, then rinse and dry them.
2. With a pin, carefully make two holes in the egg: one at the top and one at the bottom. Make the holes large enough to poke a toothpick through the egg.

3. Poke the toothpick through—this will make blowing the egg out easier. Hold the egg carefully over the bowl and place your mouth on the top hole. Blow down into the hole so that the egg white and yolk will flow out of the bottom hole and into the bowl. Do this with as many eggs as you want to decorate. You can keep the egg contents covered in the refrigerator for future use.
4. Wash the eggs again in hot water and let them dry.
5. Paint and decorate your eggs. In order to keep the egg still while you do this, poke a wooden skewer through it. You can temporarily attach the skewer with some blu-tack or scotch tape. Hold the skewer instead of the egg so you can decorate without smudging the paint.

6. After the eggs are completely dry, fold a piece of wire in half and poke it through the egg from top to bottom, folded end first. Don't put the wire all the way through, leave wire poking out of both ends. Cut about 6-8 inches of darning or embroidery thread, and thread it through the bent end of the wire, which should be on the bottom of the egg. Knot the ends of the thread so that it will not slip through the hole in the egg. You may need to insert a small piece of toothpick if the hole is too large or the thread is too narrow to make a thick enough knot. Pull the wire back through the egg.

Place your twigs in a vase, hang your decorated eggs on them, and . . . have a Happy Easter!

Herbstblätter
Fall Leaves

Germans love their forests: there are poems about them, and they are featured in books and in fairy tales such as those collected by the brothers Grimm. The city of Frankfurt even has a *Wäldchestag* (Forest Day) on which local residents go out for a picnic and celebrations in the forest.

In the 1980s, when it was discovered that the health of the German forests was suffering because of acid rain created by the emissions of cars and industry, many Germans were worried. They became interested in environmental protection, pushed for recycling programs, and joined organizations that protected the forests.

Wäldchestag. Oil painting by Heinrich Hasselhorst, 1871. Wäldchestag falls on the Tuesday after Pentecost, and is the high point of the Pentecost holiday. The city of Frankfurt has been celebrating this day for centuries. Even today, many people leave work by midday and meet up with friends and family to have a picnic in the forest and celebrate.

The most famous German forest is probably the Black Forest. This forest gets its name from the high trees that block most of the light from reaching the ground below. Many Germans enjoy walks in the woods on Sundays—about one-third of the land is covered in forest, so people don't have to travel far to reach one.

The most common species of trees in Germany are beech, pine, oak, and spruce trees. In this activity, you will make a tablecloth—perhaps with matching napkins—printing leaf patterns all along the border.

Materials

Newspaper to cover your work surface
A scrap piece of fabric
Cotton or linen tablecloth (with napkins, if desired),
    washed without softener
A collection of leaves from different trees
Fabric paint
A paint roller about 3 inches wide
    and/or a small paint brush
Plastic plates, one for each color you want to use
A brayer (available at an art supply or craft store)
Several sheets of drawing paper or parchment paper

1. Collect leaves that are flexible and won't crumble when pressure is applied to them. They should also have strong veins running on the underside.
2. Think about how you want your finished tablecloth to look. Do you prefer just a few leaves around the border, leaves throughout, stripes, or another design? A pattern of oak and maple, oak and maple, or large and small, large and small? One color of paint for all your leaves, or many different colors?
3. Spread out the newspaper and do a trial run with your fabric scrap to perfect your printing technique. Begin with the lightest color and wash the brush and paint roller between colors. Put the first color of fabric paint onto a plate, and roll the paint roller in it

to coat the roller with paint. Roll the paint roller over the rough underside of the leaf until it is covered with a thin, even layer of paint. You can also use a paint brush, but you may see the pattern of the brush strokes on your print.
4. Lay the leaf paint-side down on your scrap piece of fabric and cover it with a piece of drawing or parchment paper. Roll the

brayer evenly over the paper, then carefully lift the paper and the leaf. Practice this process until you have the results you want. You may need to adjust the amount of paint, the pressure you use, or your lifting technique.

5. Once you are happy with the results, start printing on the tablecloth. Be sure to use a clean sheet of paper for each leaf so that you don't get paint from a previous print on your tablecloth. Let the paint dry according to the directions on the fabric paint.

Laternelaufen
Lantern Procession

Saint Martin of Tours was a Roman soldier living in the fourth century who later became the third bishop of Tours in France. According to legend he saw a beggar in the wintertime without clothes or food. Martin cut his red military coat in two and gave half to the beggar to keep him warm.

November 11 is now celebrated as Saint Martin's Day and there are many traditions connected to this day in Germany. The day before Saint Martin's Day, in East Frisia, children go door to door singing songs

about Saint Martin, a custom called *Martinisingen*. In the Rhine region, people bake sweet pastries shaped like little men, called *Weckmänner*; in Sauerland, the pastries are shaped like pretzels. In some areas, a bonfire is lit to celebrate the day. Some Saint Martin's Day customs are practiced all over Germany: people eat roast goose or *Martinsgans*, and children create colorful lanterns for a lantern procession.

In this project, you will make a lantern which you could use for your own Saint Martin's Day procession, or simply use as a table centerpiece.

Large piece of strong black
   card stock paper
Transparent paper, in different colors
Pencil
Glue
Scissors
Stanley knife
Tea light or short candle
Small glass jam jar (or similarly
   sized jar)—optional
Thin wire and a stick—optional

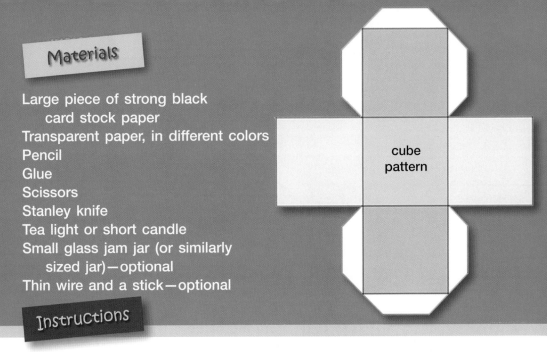

cube
pattern

Instructions

1. Draw the pattern shown onto the black card stock and cut it out.
2. On all but the center square, draw outlines of pictures which you can later cut out and line with the transparent paper. The pictures could be of Saint Martin on his horse, his sword, a cross, a bishop's hat, or any pattern you like. Be sure that you design your drawing to stay connected to the lantern once it is cut and that it is right side up—the central square will be the bottom of your lantern.

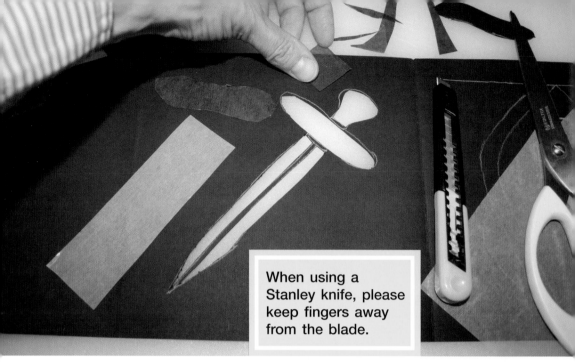

When using a
Stanley knife, please
keep fingers away
from the blade.

3. With **adult** supervision, use a Stanley knife to cut out your design. Cut the colored paper to cover the empty spaces and glue the paper to the back (inside) of the lantern. Fold the lantern and glue the flaps shut to create a cube which is open at the top. Glue the tea light to the bottom of the lantern, or (if your lantern is strong enough) insert a candle into a glass jar and place the jar inside the lantern.

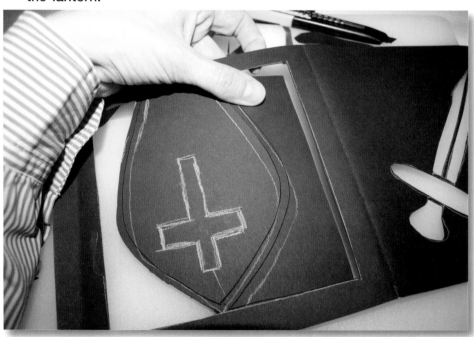

5. If you plan to use your lantern for a procession, make two holes at the top of two opposite sides of the lantern. Then, string a wire through the holes, and attach a stick. Light your candle with help from **an adult**. Never leave burning candles unattended.

Battery-operated candles can be used in place of real candles.

Adventskalender
Advent Calendar

The four weeks leading up to Christmas are known as Advent—a time of anticipation and preparation for Christmas—and are a special time particularly for children. When the days are short and cold, inside it is warm and toasty with lit candles, special crafts to decorate the house, and baking projects.

Many families put an advent wreath with four candles as a centerpiece on their dining table to mark each of the four Sundays prior to Christmas. On the first Sunday, one candle is lit, the following week two candles are lit, until all four candles are lit on the last Sunday before Christmas.

Saint Nicholas Day also falls during Advent on December 6. On Saint Nicholas Day eve, German children clean their shoes and put a pair of boots by the door in the hope that Saint Nicholas will pass by and put in a small gift and some sweets.

Most families with children also have an Advent calendar: it has twenty-four doors or containers which are opened each day starting on December 1. They can contain a spiritual message, a festive picture, a small sweet, or other little presents. There are different opinions on how old this tradition is or who invented it. Some say it was initiated by the Lutheran Church to help children count the days to Christmas.

The options are endless for making your own Advent calendar—you could use toilet paper rolls covered in festive paper or felt, cleaned yogurt containers that are decorated as Santa Claus and placed along a window, old-fashioned matchboxes decorated with tinsel, or twenty-four socks hung on the mantelpiece. This version uses little bags that you write or stitch numbers onto.

Materials

Fabric or felt
Sewing machine and thread
(or needle and thread if
sewing by hand)
Ribbon

Pins
Glue
Long string or ribbon
24 wrapped candies, or small
presents

1. Decide how large you will make your bags. Think about what you would like to put inside, and where you will hang them. They could be hung on a mantelpiece, windowsill, bookshelf, or even a refrigerator. They can be all the same size or different sizes.

2. When calculating your size, remember that your fabric will be folded in half to create the bags, and they will be ½ inch smaller around all the edges for the seam. Cut twenty-four rectangles out of the fabric or felt in the size you have calculated.

3. Fold each rectangle in two, inside out. With the assistance of **an adult**, hem along the sides, allowing ½ inch between the seam and the edge of the fabric.

4. Once they are sewn, turn the bags inside out. Depending on the stiffness of the fabric, you may want to iron the seams.

5. Cut out numbers from 1 to 24 from felt and glue or sew them onto the bags.

6. Fill each container with a candy, a gift, or a craft that you made, and tie a short ribbon to close each bag. You can tie the ribbon with a bow, or in another way so that there is a loop for hanging the bag.

7. Cut a ribbon or string that is the length that you would like your calendar to be (depending on the space you have available). Attach one end of the long ribbon to one end of your mantelpiece (or wherever you want to hang your Advent calendar). Starting with bag number 1, string the bags onto the long ribbon in order. Attach the other end of the ribbon to the far end of your mantelpiece.

8. On December 1, the recipient of your gifts can start opening one bag each morning until Christmas Eve.

Baumschmuck
Christmas Tree Ornaments

Christmas is the most important celebration in Germany. Even people who do not attend church regularly will go to church on Christmas. The story of the birth of Jesus Christ, Christmas carols, and of course presents, are all prominent features in German homes.

Another tradition which developed in Germany (possibly in order to get to the presents quickly) is to eat sausages and potato salad. In other homes, a roast goose or other roast meat is served each year.

Each family has its own traditions, but many put up, decorate, and light the Christmas tree on Christmas Eve, December 24. The Christmas tree has pagan origins, but has been in use as a symbol of Christmas since at least Medieval times. Decorations often included walnuts, apples, pretty cookies baked in shapes, paper, trinkets, tinsel, and especially candles. Although you will also find electric light strings on more environmentally-friendly reusable plastic trees, real wax candles on real trees are still used in many German homes.

Regardless of the type of tree, the decorations are often homemade. With this craft, we will make heart-shaped paper basket ornaments.

Materials

Heavy-weight paper or light card
    stock in different colors
Scissors
Glass or cup with approximately
    3 inch diameter
Glue
Pencil
Ruler

1. Measure and cut two sheets of paper in different colors in a 3 x 9 inch rectangular shape.
2. Fold the two sheets in half. Use a glass, small bowl, or anything round to trace the rounded top at the ends of the rectangle (the open side, not the folded side). Cut around the lines you've drawn.
3. Cut two slits into the folded edges of the papers, each 1 inch apart. The slits should be 3 inches long (or as long as the strip is wide).

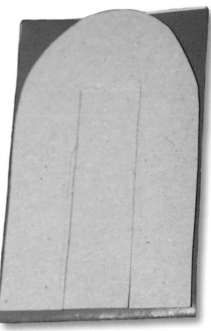

4. Using the photo as a guide, lay the two papers so that you can weave the strips as shown. Lay the folded edge of one sheet against the long side of the other sheet. Insert the innermost strip of "sheet one" inside the strip it is touching on "sheet two." Then open the slit strip of sheet one and insert the center strip of sheet two inside this opening. Finally, insert the strip from sheet one into the last and outer strip of sheet two.

5. With the center strip of sheet one, do exactly the opposite to create the weaving effect. (Begin by inserting the first strip of sheet two into the center strip of sheet one).

6. Using one of the colors you used for the heart, cut an 8-inch-long strip. Fold it over to create a handle and glue it to the inside of your heart. Your basket is ready to be hung on the tree!

Frikadellen
German Meatballs

Meat is an important food in Germany, both in terms of production and consumption. The average German consumed about 134 pounds (61 kilograms) of meat in 2010.

Frikadellen are also known as *Buletten* or *Fleischklopse* and belong to the meatball family. In Germany, they are usually eaten with some form of potato and a sauteed vegetable, like carrots. Some people also enjoy them cold!

Prepare this recipe with help from **an adult.**

Ingredients

1 day-old white bread roll
½ to 1 cup of milk
½ pound of pork, minced
½ pound of beef, minced
1 egg
1 tablespoon mustard
Salt, pepper, nutmeg, and parsley, to taste
2-3 tablespoons oil

Instructions

Serves: 6-8

1. Place the bread in a bowl and cover it with milk. Allow it to soak for a few minutes.
2. Squeeze out any excess milk, then put the mushy bread in a large mixing bowl. Add all of the other ingredients except for the oil, and mix well with your hands.
3. Wet your hands with cold water and form flattened patties the size of the palm of your hand.

4. Put the oil in the pan over medium heat. Fry the meatballs in the oil for approximately 6 minutes, then flip them over and cook for 6 or 7 minutes longer. Depending on the size of your pan, you may need to do this in several batches.

Serve with boiled or mashed potatoes, and a salad or sauteed vegetable of your choice.

Senfeier
Eggs in Mustard

This is a very simple and satisfying egg recipe probably from Saxony-Anhalt, an eastern German state.

Prepare this recipe with the help of **an adult**.

Ingredients

Serves: 8-10 (as a side)
Serves: 3-4 (as a meal)

2 pounds potatoes
Salt
8 eggs
4 tablespoons Dijon mustard (or to taste)
6 tablespoons butter
4 tablespoons flour
2 cups chicken stock or milk
Salt, pepper

Instructions

1. Wash and peel the potatoes, and cut them into 1-inch pieces. Boil them in salted water until soft—about 20 minutes. Prick the potatoes with a fork to see if they are cooked through—if the fork cuts through easily, they are ready. Drain them and set aside.
2. While you wait for the potatoes to cook, place the eggs in a pot, and cover them with cold water. Add salt, and bring the water to a boil on the stove, and then turn off the heat and cover. Allow the eggs to cook in the hot water for 10-15 minutes if you like them hard boiled, or 5-6 minutes if you like them a bit softer. When the eggs are cooked, hold them under cold water and peel the shells. Set aside.
3. To make the sauce, heat the broth or milk until it is warm and set aside. Melt the butter in a pot over medium heat and whisk in the flour. Keep stirring with the whisk for 4-5 minutes. Remove the pot from the heat, and very slowly add a small ladleful of hot broth (or milk) to the butter-flour mixture, continuing to whisk. After the first

ladleful of broth or milk has been mixed in well, add another portion of broth or milk, whisking the entire time. Continue until all the broth or milk has been used up. Return the pot to low heat, and stir until you have a dense, sauce-like consistency (about 5 minutes). Don't stop stirring or you will get a very lumpy sauce.

4. Turn the stove off and season the sauce with salt, pepper, and mustard.

5. Cut the eggs in half, and place on a plate with the potatoes. Pour the sauce over the eggs and potatoes, and serve.

Osterzopf
Easter Bread

Germans love their Easter Sunday breakfast or brunch. This is one of the typical breads served during this festive meal.

You can also add washed hard boiled eggs in their shell to braid before putting it into the oven to make it look even more festive.

This recipe requires some time for the *Zopf* (bread) to rise. You will need a warm, draft-free place such as an oven with only the light switched on. Prepare this recipe with the help of **an adult**.

Ingredients

⅓ cup milk
2 cups all-purpose flour
2 packages dry yeast
¼ cup plus 2 tablespoons sugar
6 tablespoons butter
Grated rind of ½ lemon
1 large egg
1 egg white
½ cup raisins (optional)

1 egg yolk
1 tablespoon milk
A handful of sliced almonds and/or coarse sugar

Instructions

1. Mix the flour with sugar, salt, and yeast in a large mixing bowl.
2. Melt the butter. In a separate pan, heat the milk gently until it is lukewarm—you should

be able to hold your clean finger in without burning. Add the melted butter, warm milk, lemon rind, the egg, and the egg white into the flour mix.

3. Knead well until the dough is smooth. If it is too dry you can add milk, and if it is too moist, add flour. If you are using raisins, add them and knead some more so that they are evenly distributed.

4. Cover the dough with a clean towel and let it rest in a warm, draft-free place until the size is doubled. This should take about 1 hour.

5. Knead the dough again briefly and divide it into three equal parts. Roll the three sections into long strands. Pinch the ends of the three strands together, and braid them, pinching again at the other end. Let the loaf rest again for 30 minutes.

6. Preheat the oven to 350°F.

7. Beat the egg yolk together with the milk, and coat the Zopf with the mix using a pastry brush. Sprinkle with almonds and coarse sugar and bake it for about 40 minutes.

Forelle Blau
Blue Trout

A German fish recipe could easily be a salmon recipe, as it is one of the most common types of fish eaten in the country. Herring has a very long culinary and economic history in Germany. Trout is also very popular, and in the United States, is both easier to find and easier on most palates. Plus, the fish in this recipe turns color when handled correctly, giving it its name.

Prepare this recipe with the help of **an adult.**

Ingredients

Serves: 6

3 quarts water
2 onions
2 tablespoons salt
1 teaspoon juniper berries (available at a specialty or natural foods store)
1 teaspoon black peppercorns
3 bay leaves
1 carrot
1 small piece of leek
1 stick celery
3 gutted rainbow trouts
1 cup white wine vinegar

Note: Be careful to touch the fish with wet hands only—if you scale or damage the skin of the fish, it will not turn blue.

Instructions

1. Peel the onions and carrot. Wash the leek and celery well, and cut all vegetables into 1-inch pieces.
2. In a large pot, add water together with the salt, berries, peppercorns, bay leaves and vegetables,

and bring to a boil. Turn the heat to low, cover the pot, and let simmer for about 30 minutes.

3. In the meantime, wash the trout carefully and sprinkle salt on the insides. Lay the fish in a pan where they can lie flat next to each other.

4. Bring the vinegar to a boil in a small pot or in the microwave. Pour the vinegar over the fish in the pan.

5. Place a large sieve over the pan, and slowly pour the hot broth into it. Discard the contents of the sieve, cover the pot, and let simmer at the lowest temperature for 10-12 minutes.

Serve with potatoes, hot butter, and a green salad on the side.

Rote Grütze
Red Berry Dessert

One of the best things about summer in Germany is the variety of berries and soft fruit available. Sometimes you can pick the fruit yourself, and you can also find it at local markets. *Grütze* originated in Northern Germany, but today it is popular all over Germany. It is a wonderful cooling summer dessert.

Prepare this recipe with the help of an **adult.**

Ingredients

Serves: 4-6

3 cups mixed berries (strawberries, black and red currants, raspberries, blackberries, blueberries), fresh or frozen
3 tablespoons sugar, or to taste
1 teaspoon grated lemon peel
1 cup black currant juice (available at natural foods stores; if you can't find black currant juice, you can also use grape juice)
2 tablespoons cornstarch
Water

Instructions

1. Put all ingredients except the cornstarch in a pot and bring to a boil. Lower the heat and simmer for about 5-10 minutes—the fruit should not dissolve completely.
2. In a small bowl, mix the cornstarch with a bit of cold water until the starch is completely dissolved. Add this paste to the fruit, stirring continuously.
3. Bring to a boil one more time, then pour in a bowl, allow to cool, and put the Grütze in the refrigerator for a few hours or overnight.

Serve with vanilla sauce or vanilla ice cream.

Rouladen
Rolled Beef

The Sunday roast is also a German tradition. In the South, it is often eaten with dumplings or small noodles called *Spätzle*. In other parts of the country, it may be eaten with potatoes and a vegetable side dish, usually stewed red cabbage.

Prepare this recipe with the help of **an adult**.

Ingredients

Serves: 6

6 slices top round (about 4 x 6 inches, and ⅜ inch thick)
3 slices lean bacon
½ onion, sliced
3 pickles, sliced
Mustard, salt, pepper
2 tablespoons butter
1-2 cups water
1 onion, chopped finely
1 carrot, chopped finely
1 stick of celery, chopped
Kitchen string or toothpicks
1 tablespoon cornstarch

Instructions

1. Cover one slice of meat with plastic wrap so your meat doesn't splatter. Gently pound the meat with the flat side of a meat mallet (or other flat utensil) until it is evenly thick, about ⅛ inch. Be careful not to put holes in the meat. Repeat with the other slices.
2. Lay the slices out on your work surface and spread mustard, salt, and pepper on them.

3. At one end of the meat slice, lay half a piece of bacon, slices of half a pickle, and a few pieces of sliced onion.

4. Carefully roll up the meat, starting from the end with the filling.

Tie the rolled up meat with kitchen string, or use 2 toothpicks to fasten the rolls so they don't fall apart in the frying process. Salt and pepper them from the outside.

5. Heat the oil on medium-high heat in a pan and fry two or three Rouladen until they are brown on all sides. Do not put too many into the pan as they will not brown properly. Take out the Rouladen and put them on a plate. Repeat with the others.

6. Return all Rouladen to the pan; add the chopped onion, carrot, celery, and a cup of hot water. Turn down the heat and let simmer, covered, for one hour and a half. Take out all the Rouladen.

7. In a small bowl, mix a tablespoon of cornstarch with just enough cold water to make a paste. Add the cornstarch mix to the bubbling sauce. Return the meat to the pot and add some sour cream for a rounder flavor. Cook a few minutes longer, then discard the vegetables and serve.

Apfelkuchen
Apple Cake

Traditionally a small meal of cake and coffee, tea, or hot chocolate was served at home in the afternoon. Due to changes in work patterns, this has been relegated to the weekend for most people, however a huge selection of cakes, cookies, and other sweet pastries is still available. These are either baked in the home or bought in the bakery or pastry shop (*Konditorei*). Cake is often served with whipped cream.

Here is a recipe for a typical German apple cake or *Apfelkuchen*. Prepare this recipe with the help of **an adult**.

Ingredients

10 ⅔ tablespoons butter, room temperature
½ cup sugar
1¼ cups all-purpose flour
2 eggs
1 teaspoon vanilla extract
½ teaspoon salt
2-3 tablespoons ground almonds
1 teaspoon cinnamon
5-6 apples
1 lemon, or lemon juice

Glaze
2 eggs
4 tablespoons sour cream
2 tablespoons sugar
2 tablespoons raisins (optional)

Instructions

1. Preheat the oven to 350°F.
2. Make a dough by putting the first six ingredients in a large mixing bowl and mixing until well combined.
3. Butter a 10-inch round baking pan.

4. Peel, core, and slice the apples to ¼ inch thickness, then sprinkle the apples with lemon juice so they do not discolor.

5. Pour the dough into the baking pan and sprinkle with the almonds. Lay the apples on top and sprinkle with cinnamon. Bake for about 40 minutes.

6. While the cake is baking, prepare the glaze by mixing the eggs, sour cream, sugar, and the raisins (if you are using them). Once the cake has baked for 40 minutes, pour this mixture over the half-baked cake and bake for an additional 20 minutes.

Serve with whipped cream

Würste & Sauerkraut
Sausages and Sauerkraut

Sausages are another of the many German meat products. Regional specialties include Weisswürste (white veal sausages from Bavara in the South), Frankfurter (from Frankfurt), Nürnberger Bratwurst (from Nuremberg), Thüringer Bratwurst (from Thuringia), Grützwurst (blood sausage), or Currywurst (from Berlin). All are well known and popular in Germany.

Sauerkraut is a vegetable dish that is eaten regularly in most of the country. Made with the humble white cabbage, it has a long tradition all over central Europe and provided much-needed vitamins and other nutrients in the winter time before the era of refrigeration.

Prepare this recipe with the help of **an adult.**

Ingredients

Serves: 4

1 onion
1 tablespoon oil
1 tablespoon brown sugar
½–1 teaspoon sugar or honey, according to taste
2 cups sauerkraut
1 cup chicken or vegetable broth
1 bay leaf
4 juniper berries (available at a specialty food or natural food store)
8 sausages or cured pork (any kind you like)

Instructions

1. Rinse the sauerkraut. Peel and finely chop the onion.
2. Heat the oil in a medium saucepan over medium heat and gently fry the onion until it is translucent. Don't let it brown. Sprinkle the onion with a tablespoon of brown sugar. Let the sugar dissolve or even caramelize, but don't let it get too dark or it will taste bitter. Adding the additional sugar (or honey) will help to make the dish a bit milder.

3. Add the sauerkraut, broth, bay leaf, and juniper berries, and heat it through. Don't add salt because the sauerkraut and sausages are both quite salty.
4. Now add the sausages, cover the pan, and cook over medium-low heat for at least 20 minutes, or until the sausages are cooked through.

Serve with mashed or boiled potatoes.

Vanillekipferl
Vanilla Christmas Cookies

Christmas time starts four weeks before Christmas and is a time of *Christkindlmarkets* (Christmas Markets), wrapping presents, creating decorations for the Christmas tree or the nativity, and, of course, baking. *Lebkuchen* (a gingerbread-like biscuit), *Stollen* (fruit cake), *Zimtsterne* (cinnamon star cookies), *Pfefferkuchen* (spice cookies), and many other regional and national specialties are often made in the home and given as presents to friends, teachers, colleagues, and family. The following recipe is for *Vanillekipferl* which are originally Austrian, but are so popular and omnipresent at Christmas in Germany that a German recipe collection would not be complete without them.

Prepare this recipe with the help of **an adult**.

Ingredients

½ cup sugar
2 cups all-purpose flour
1 cup and 1 tablespoon
    butter
½ cup ground almonds
3 teaspoons vanilla
    sugar (available at a
    specialty food or
    natural food store; if
    you can't find it, you
    can also add a dash
    of vanilla extract to
    3 teaspoons of white
    sugar)
1 egg
3-4 tablespoons
    confectioners' sugar

1. Put the first six ingredients into a large mixing bowl and knead to make a smooth dough. Cover with plastic wrap and put it in the refrigerator for one hour.
2. Preheat the oven to 350°F.

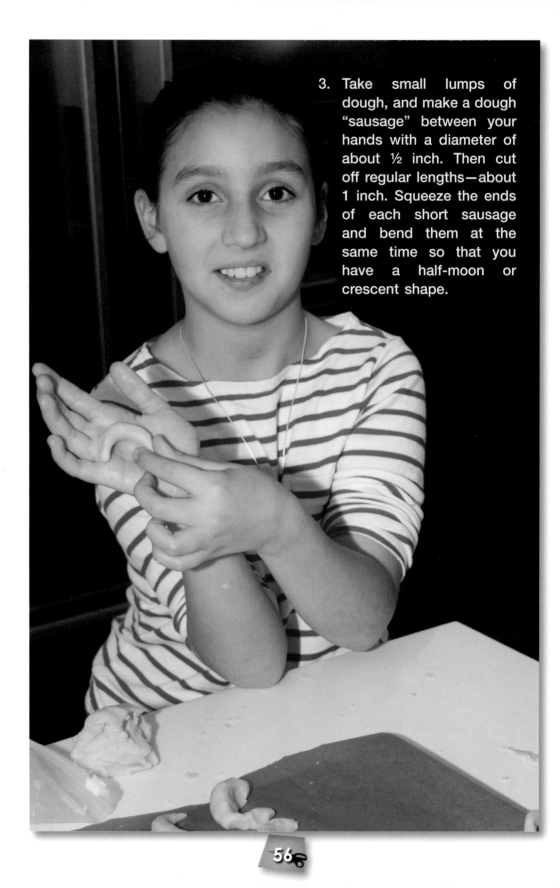

3. Take small lumps of dough, and make a dough "sausage" between your hands with a diameter of about ½ inch. Then cut off regular lengths—about 1 inch. Squeeze the ends of each short sausage and bend them at the same time so that you have a half-moon or crescent shape.

4. Lay them on a baking sheet that is greased or covered in parchment paper.
5. Bake the cookies for about 10 minutes. Take them out of the oven and sieve some confectioners' sugar on them while they are still warm.

You can keep these in an airtight container for a few weeks—if you can resist!

Makes about 3 dozen cookies.

Abendbrot
German Dinner

Bread is a mainstay of German cuisine. Traditionally, two of the three main meals of the day consisted of bread with something else: breakfast was bread with butter and jam or honey, and dinner was so-called *Abendbrot*, or "evening bread": bread with cheese, cold cuts, pickles, salad, etc. Because of this, bakeries can still be found in every village and shopping street. It is said that there are over 300 varieties of German bread.

The bread is also the reason why most supermarkets and independent butcher shops carry a huge array of cold cuts—the bread has to be eaten with something on it! Fifteen hundred varieties of sausage are produced in Germany today.

German politician Otto von Bismarck famously said: "The less people know about how sausages and laws are made, the better they'll sleep at night."

This German dinner doesn't require cooking, but does require some planning and arranging.

If you have access to a kosher deli you will find things which come very close to what you might buy in Germany.

Ingredients

Pickles
Mustard
An array of breads: pumpernickel, cracker bread, rye bread, etc.
Quark cheese (if not available at your local grocery store, you can
   also try mixing two parts ricotta cheese to one part sour cream)
Slices of cucumber, tomatoes, radishes
Pâté
Any kind of cold cut: ham, salami, turkey, etc.
Any kind of cheese
Smoked fish
Egg salad
Butter
Salt and pepper and chopped chives (to sprinkle on the quark)

Arrange the food on platters and serving dishes, and invite your friends for a big feast!

milfina
Speisequark

Further Reading

Books

Byers, Ann. *Germany: A Primary Source Cultural Guide.* New York: The Rosen Publishing Group, Inc., 2005.

Childress, Diana. *Johannes Gutenberg and the Printing Press.* Minneapolis: Twenty-First Century Books, 2008.

Sheen, Barbara. *Foods of Germany.* Farmington Hills, MI: Gale, 2006.

Townsend, Sue. *A World of Recipes: Germany.* Chicago: Heinemann/Raintree, 2003.

Works Consulted

Delea: German Culture
http://www.deutsche-lebensart.de

Essen & Trinken
http://www.essen-und-trinken.de

German Missions in Australia
http://www.canberra.diplo.de/Vertretung/canberra/de/06/Feste__Traditionen__Lebenstil/Feste__Traditionen__Lebenstil.html

Gutenberg: Man of the Millennium, "Gutenberg's Invention"
http://www.gutenberg.de/english/erfindun.htm

Harzlife, "Walpurgisnacht—History and Background Knowledge"
http://www.harzlife.de/event/walpurgis-info.html

Marions Kochbuck
http://www.marions-kochbuch.com

Quick German Recipes
http://www.quick-german-recipes.com/index.html

Statistisches Bundesamt (Federal Statistical Office)
http://www.destatis.de

The Artful Parent
http://artfulparent.typepad.com/artfulparent/

Zentralverband des Deutschen Bäckerhandwerks e. V. (National Federation of Bakers)
http://www.baeckerhandwerk.de

On the Internet
DE Magazine Deutschland
> http://www.deutschland.de/en
Facts About Germany
> http://www.tatsachen-ueber-deutschland.de/en/
MyGermanCity.com: "Germany—Historical Places, Modern Culture"
> http://www.mygermancity.com/germany

PHOTO CREDITS: Cover, pp. 2–3, 4, 8, 9, 12, 14, 16, 20, 22, 32, 34–35, 38, 46, 59, 61—Photos.com; pp. 10, 11, 13, 15, 17, 18, 19, 21, 23, 25, 26, 27, 28, 29, 30, 31, 33, 39, 40, 41, 42, 43, 44, 45, 47, 48, 49, 50, 51, 53—Julia Harms; p. 24—Heinrich Hasselhorst; pp. 35, 36, 37, 54, 55, 56, 57— Kristina Thiele. Every effort has been made to locate all copyright holders of material used in this book. If any errors or omissions have occurred, corrections will be made in future editions of the book.

Glossary

Advent—The four Sundays leading up to Christmas.

Allies, Allied Forces —The countries that opposed Nazi Germany and the Axis forces in World War II. These countries included France, Britain, the United States, and the Soviet Union.

Black Death—Epidemic of a form of the bubonic plague, a bacterial disease that killed millions throughout Europe in the fourteenth century.

capitalism—An economic system in which resources and means of production are privately owned and prices, production, and the distribution of goods are determined mainly by competition in a free market.

cold war—A rivalry over political differences (as between two nations), which occurs without military conflict and usually without breaking off of diplomatic relations.

communism—A social system in which property and goods are owned in common.

cuisine—Style of cooking; the food cooked.

European Union—Powerful economic and political union of twenty-seven member states in Europe.

Holocaust—The mass murder of Jewish people ordered by the German government during World War II.

industrial revolution—A rapid major change in an economy marked by the general introduction of power-driven machinery.

kosher—Accepted by Jewish law; selling or serving food ritually fit according to Jewish law.

medieval—Referring to the Middle Ages.

Middle Ages—A period in European history that lasted roughly from the sixth century CE to the fifteenth century CE. It was also called the Dark Ages.

pagan—Referring to any religion that is not Christian, Jewish, or Muslim, often a religion which honors more than one god.

palate—The sense of taste.

socialism—Any of various social systems based on shared or governmental ownership and administration of the means of production and distribution of goods.

Soviet Union—The union of several states (including Russia) into a single socialist nation that existed between 1922 and 1991.

unification—The process of making into a single unit or a whole.

Index

ABOUT THE
AUTHOR

Julia Harms was born and grew up in Hamburg, Germany. After high school, she went to explore the world beyond Germany and lived in the United States, England, Italy, and China amongst others. She is married with three children, and recently settled in Switzerland. Crafting and cooking with and for her family is one of the things she likes best. German celebrations such as the lantern procession, St. Nicholas, and Easter egg hunts are celebrated wherever she lives. She has also written *Recipe and Craft Guide to Italy*.